Cambridge **Discovery Education**™

▶ **INTERACTIVE READERS**

Series editor: Bob Hastings

FEEDING TIME
THE FEEDING HABITS
OF ANIMALS

A1⁺

Theo Walker

CAMBRIDGE
UNIVERSITY PRESS

Discovery
EDUCATION™

CAMBRIDGE UNIVERSITY PRESS
Cambridge, New York, Melbourne, Madrid, Cape Town,
Singapore, São Paulo, Delhi, Mexico City

Cambridge University Press
32 Avenue of the Americas, New York, NY 10013-2473, USA

www.cambridge.org
Information on this title: www.cambridge.org/9781107678675

© Cambridge University Press 2014

First published 2014

Printed in Hong Kong, China, by Golden Cup Printing Company Limited

A catalog record for this publication is available from the British Library.

Library of Congress Cataloging-in-Publication Data

Walker, Theo.
 Feeding time : the feeding habits of animals / Theo Walker.
   pages cm. -- (Cambridge discovery interactive readers)
 ISBN 978-1-107-67867-5 (pbk. : alk. paper)
 1. Animal feeding--Juvenile literature. 2. English language--Textbooks for foreign speakers.
 3. Readers (Elementary) I. Title.

SF95.W25 2013
636.08'4--dc23

                              2013021185

ISBN 978-1-107-67867-5

Additional resources for this publication at www.cambridge.org

Layout services, art direction, book design, and photo research: Q2ABillSMITH GROUP
Editorial services: Hyphen S.A.
Audio production: CityVox, New York
Video production: Q2ABillSMITH GROUP

Contents

Before You Read: Get Ready! 4

CHAPTER 1
Eat to Live 6

CHAPTER 2
The Mouth 8

CHAPTER 3
The Stomach 12

CHAPTER 4
Waste 16

CHAPTER 5
What Do You Think? 20

After You Read 22

Answer Key 24

Glossary

Before You Read:
Get Ready!

What happens after we eat food? What does the body do with the food we eat? Let's take a look at the body to find out!

Match the words with their definitions. Then use the words to label the parts on the picture.

1 stomach   **a** the hard white things you use to chew food

2 teeth   **b** the part of the head that is used for eating

3 tongue   **c** where the food changes into energy

4 mouth   **d** the soft thing inside your mouth that can move around

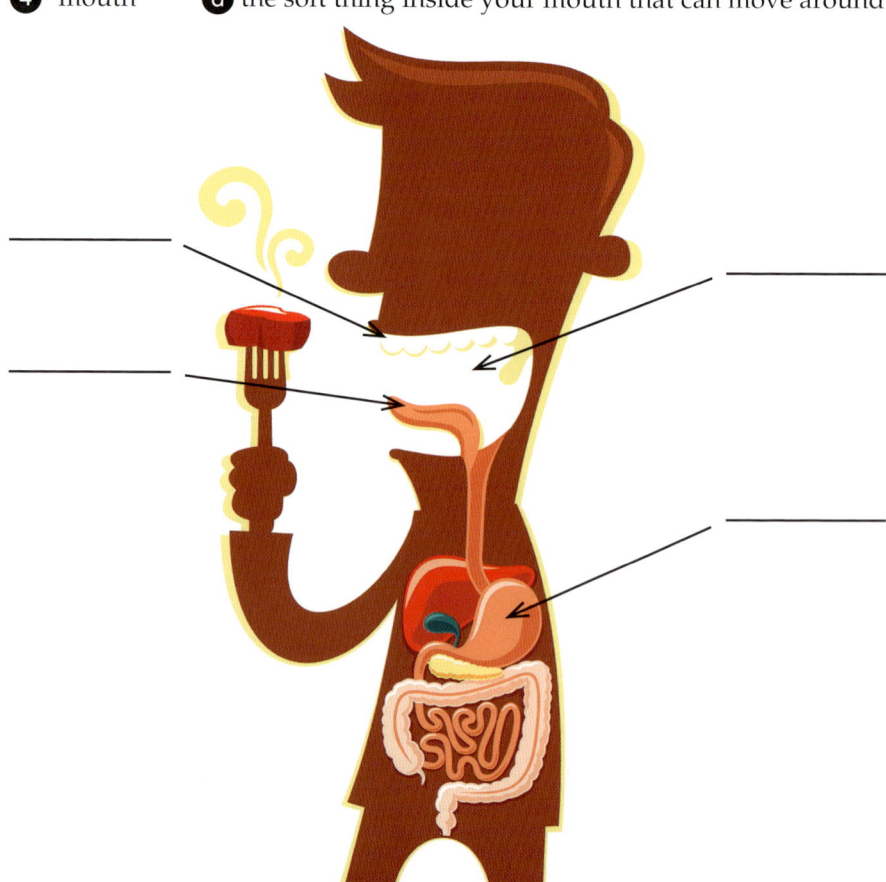

Words to Know

Read the paragraph. Then complete the sentences with the correct highlighted words.

To digest food is to change food into what we need. First, we use our teeth to bite the food and get it in our mouth. Then, we chew the food to make it smaller. The tongue moves the food and makes it into a ball. The water in the mouth is called saliva. Together, the teeth, tongue, and saliva change the food so it is ready to swallow. After we swallow the food, it goes to the stomach. The stomach digests the food, so the body can get energy from it. We need energy to move and live. But the body does not need some parts of the food. When those parts leave the body, they are called waste.

1 When food is ready to leave the mouth, we _____ it.

2 The _____ moves the food in the mouth.

3 To _____ food is to make it ready for the body to use.

4 Food goes into the _____ after it leaves the mouth.

5 Without _____ we can't live and move.

6 _____ is the food the body doesn't need.

7 We _____ food to get it into our mouth.

8 We _____ food to make it smaller.

9 The water in the mouth is called _____.

CHAPTER 1

Eat to Live

**EVERY LIVING THING NEEDS FOOD.
WHAT DOES THE BODY DO WITH FOOD?
WHAT DOES FOOD DO FOR THE BODY?**

All animals need to eat food. The food gives them energy to run, fly, live, and **grow**. But how much do different animals eat? Some animals need to eat more than others. Most birds need a lot of food. They eat from half to all of their weight[1] in a day. For

A bird brings food to babies in the nest.

example, a bird that weighs two kilograms eats one to two kilograms of food. **Scientists** watched one bird bring food back to her babies 1,200 times in one day!

[1] **weigh/weight (verb/noun):** how heavy something is

Koalas weigh 5–14 kilograms. They are not large animals, but for how much they weigh, they don't eat very much. They only eat about 1.3 kilograms of leaves from the eucalyptus tree a day. The leaves don't have

Koalas eat eucalyptus leaves.

many nutrients.[2] Koalas sleep 16 to 18 hours a day because the leaves don't give them much energy.

Bears often sleep all the time in the winter. Before the bears go to sleep, they must eat a lot of food. They can eat 40 kilograms of food in the week before they go to sleep. They need to get very fat because they can't eat when they are sleeping! When they sleep, the fat becomes energy. Without this energy, the bears can't live through the winter.

And some big animals eat a lot all year. At night, a hippopotamus leaves the river where it sleeps most of the day. It eats plants and grasses for about five hours. It eats about 40 kilograms of food a night.

[2]**nutrient:** the part of food that helps bodies live and grow

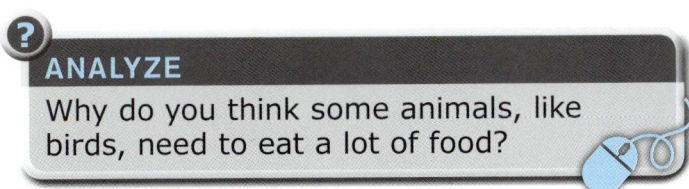

? ANALYZE

Why do you think some animals, like birds, need to eat a lot of food?

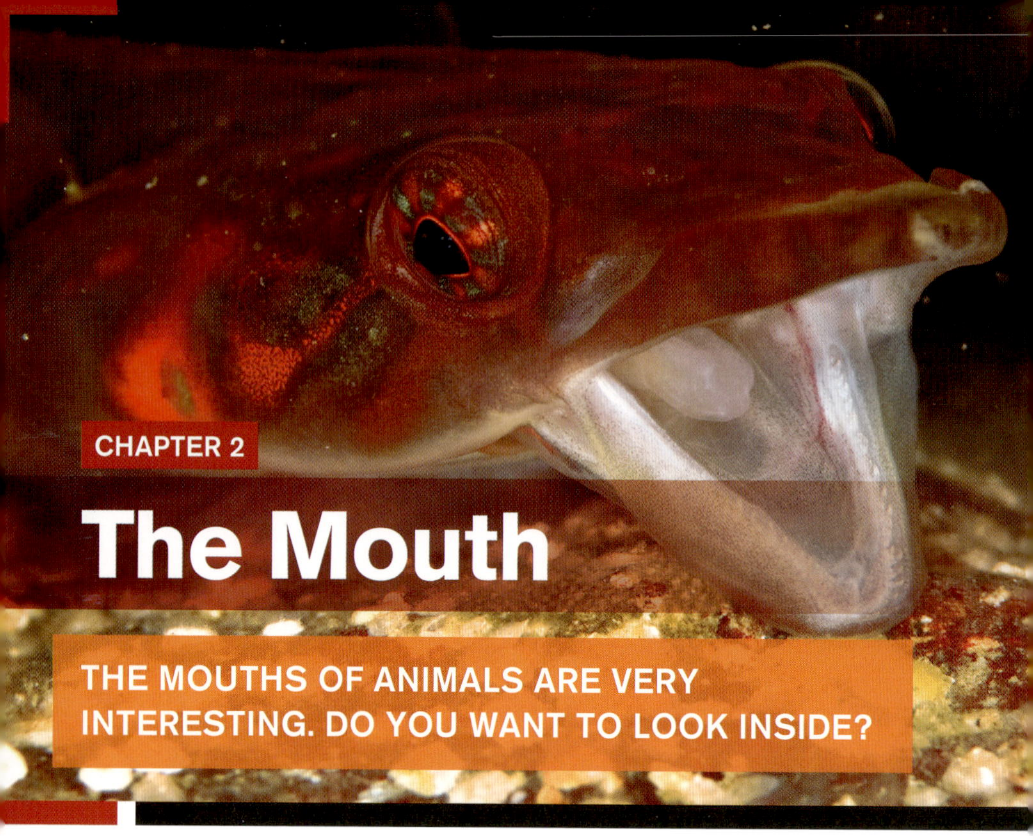

CHAPTER 2

The Mouth

THE MOUTHS OF ANIMALS ARE VERY INTERESTING. DO YOU WANT TO LOOK INSIDE?

Sucker fish get their name from their mouths. They use their mouths to suck[3] food into their bodies. People with pet fish sometimes use sucker fish to clean the water for their fish. The sucker fish sucks and eats the very small things in the water to make it clean.

The mouth of a bird is called a beak. One kind of hummingbird has a beak that is longer than its body! The hummingbird's beak goes down into flowers to drink the juice. Inside the beak is a long, slim **tongue** that gets the juice out of the flower.

[3]**suck:** use air to make something move into the mouth

A hummingbird

The chameleon's tongue is longer than its body. The chameleon moves its long tongue quickly out of its mouth to catch insects.[4] The tongue then brings the insects into the chameleon's mouth.

A chameleon

The tongue of the blue whale is so big that 50 people can stand on it! Whales eat a lot. The blue whale eats more than 3,000 kilograms of fish every day. First, it takes a big drink of water and catches a lot of fish in its mouth. Then its big tongue pushes the water out through little spaces[5] under its mouth. The fish can't get out. Then the whale eats all the fish.

....

[4] **insect:** a small animal with six legs
[5] **space:** an empty place

Blue whales

?

EVALUATE

Which animal eats in the most interesting way? Why do you think so?

A shark

Many sharks have 40 to 90 **teeth**. The whale shark, however, has thousands of teeth! Sharks' teeth are dangerous. They're long and sharp like knives. They use their teeth to **kill** fish and other animals. When a shark loses a tooth, a new tooth grows in the space. A shark can have more than 30,000 teeth in its life!

Snakes use their teeth to catch animals, but they don't use their teeth to eat. First, the snake opens its mouth, so it's very big. Then the snake swallows all of the animal without **chewing**! A snake can eat animals that are much bigger than it is!

A snake

Gila monster

Komodo dragon

Saliva makes it easier for animals to swallow their food. But it also helps some animals catch their food. The Gila monster and the Komodo dragon are lizards.[6] They both have saliva with poison[7] in it. After a Gila monster or Komodo dragon bites an animal, the poison makes the animal sick. Soon, it stops moving, and the lizard can eat it. The Gila monster eats eggs, insects, smaller lizards, and other small animals. The Komodo dragon can kill and eat very big animals, even pigs, horses, or people!

[6] **lizard:** a small animal with a long tail and four short legs
[7] **poison:** something that makes you sick or kills you

Video Quest

Komodo Dragons

Watch this video to learn about the Komodo dragon. What is the most important difference between the Gila monster and the Komodo dragon?

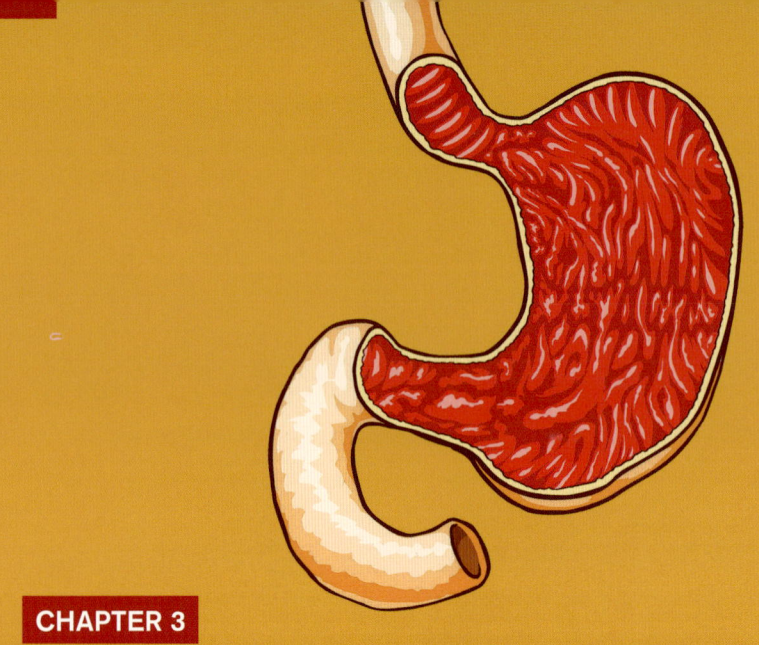

CHAPTER 3

The Stomach

FOOD CHANGES INTO ENERGY IN THE STOMACH. DO YOU KNOW WHY ANIMALS HAVE DIFFERENT KINDS OF STOMACHS?

After an animal chews and swallows, the food travels to the **stomach**. The stomach does most of the work of **digesting** the food. A liquid[8] comes out of the walls of the stomach. This liquid has important things in it that take nutrients out of the food. These nutrients give the body energy. Most animals have stomachs. Some animals have stomachs with several parts. And other animals have no stomach!

[8]**liquid:** anything wet, like water or saliva

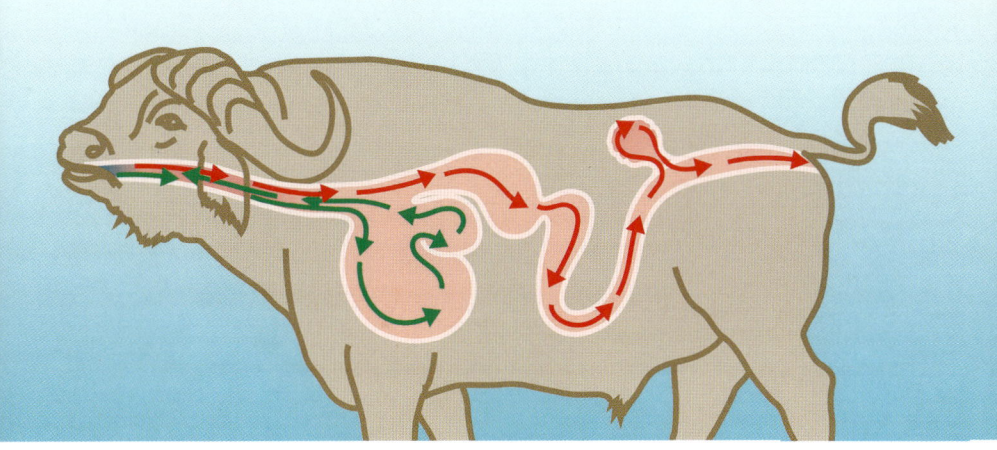

The cow's stomach

The cow's stomach is different from ours. It has four parts. Why is this? Well, a cow eats a lot of grass quickly. First, the cow swallows the grass but does not chew it very much. This food goes into the first part of the stomach. Later, parts of this food, called the cud, go back up to the mouth of the cow. The cow chews the cud and swallows it down again. The cud can go up and down 40 to 60 times! Then, the other parts of the stomach digest the cud.

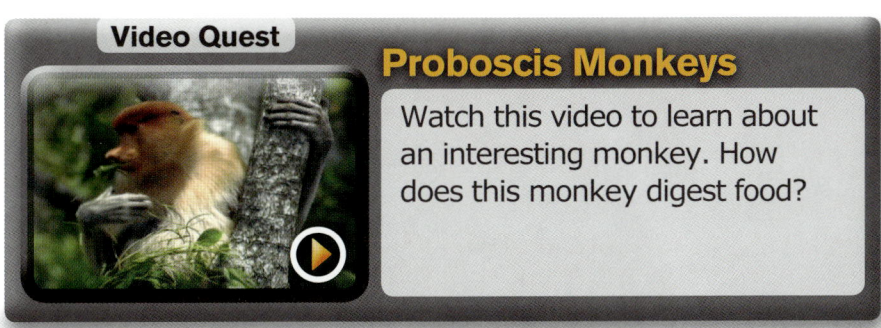

Video Quest

Proboscis Monkeys

Watch this video to learn about an interesting monkey. How does this monkey digest food?

A seahorse is a beautiful little animal that lives in the deep waters of the ocean. Seahorses have no stomach at all! They also have no teeth. Seahorses eat very small fish. They suck and swallow the fish without chewing.

Seahorses

How much time does the stomach of an animal need to digest its food? Some animals need a lot of time because of the kind of food they eat. For example, a dog eats a lot of meat. The stomach of a dog needs to work a lot to digest this kind of food. A dog's stomach needs about eight hours to digest meat.

But birds that eat fruit are different. These birds only need 30–60 minutes to digest fruit. And what about seahorses? They suck in water with fish into their mouths. They have no stomach, so the food goes out again very quickly. They need to eat all the time!

CHAPTER 4

Waste

HOW CAN SOMETHING SO BAD BE SO GOOD?

An animal's body takes some nutrients out of food. The rest is **waste**. Animal waste is dirty, and it must leave the body so the animal does not get sick. But animal waste has other nutrients in it. These nutrients are good for the soil.[9] Farmers use dung – the waste from animals that eat grass – to help grow plants.

People also use animal waste, dead plants, and old food to make compost. Compost is like dung – full of nutrients for the soil. People use compost in their gardens to make the soil better. It helps them grow vegetables, plants, and flowers.

[9]**soil:** plants grow in the soil

The waste of zoo animals is also very good for the soil. Today, zoos sell waste to farmers and gardeners. For example, Zoo Miami in Florida, USA, gets 635 kilograms of waste from elephants, 340 kilograms from rhinoceroses, and 226 kilograms from giraffes every day! These animals also eat grass, so their dung is good for the soil.

Maybe someone you know uses elephant dung to grow their flowers or food!

ANALYZE

How are cow dung, compost, and zoo animal waste the same?

Zoos sell the dung of elephants, giraffes, and rhinoceroses to farmers.

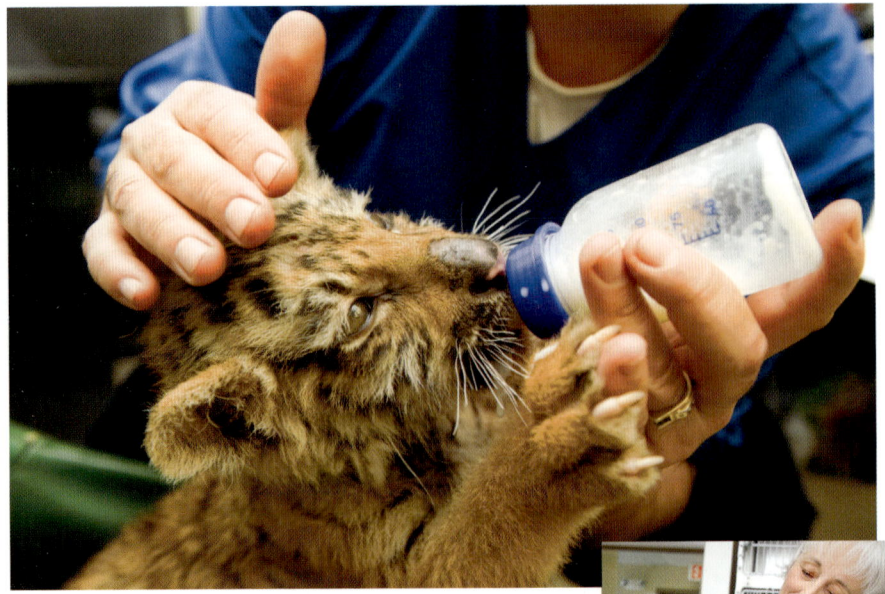

There are many other good things about animal waste. Animal doctors, or **veterinarians**, and scientists learn a lot from studying scat. Scat is another name for animal waste, and it shows what an animal ate. Scat also shows what things the animal did not digest.

Animals often get sick when they eat something bad. A veterinarian can study an animal's scat to learn what bad things it ate and why it is sick. Scientists use scat to learn about wild[10] animals: how they live, how far they travel, and if they have enough food and water.

[10]**wild:** not a pet

Did you know that some animals can eat their waste and not get sick? Rabbits, for example, eat their own waste. It has a lot of undigested plants in it, so it's like food for them. Baby koalas eat their mother's waste. Waste has bacteria[11] in it. A lot of bacteria in waste is bad and can make animals sick. But there are also good kinds of

bacteria that help with digestion. Baby koalas do not have enough of the good bacteria in their bodies, so they need to eat their mother's waste to get it.

[11]**bacteria:** very small living things that can make people or animals sick

Video Quest

Tiger Scat

Watch this video to find about the scat, or *tati*, of a tiger. What do the people learn from it?

CHAPTER 5

What Do You Think?

HERE ARE SOME SAYINGS[12] THAT COME FROM EATING AND DIGESTING.

Some people say, "Don't live to eat, eat to live," because they think that many of us eat too much or think about eating too much. Do you think people eat too much? What about you and the people you know? Do you think animals eat too much sometimes?

When people think about or see something that is really good to eat, they say "it makes my mouth water." When we think about or see something good to eat, our mouth makes saliva so we can swallow the food. What food makes your mouth water?

[12]**saying:** famous words people say about life

You know that cows chew their cud 40 to 60 times. But when people say that they are going to "chew their cud," then they are going to think about something a lot. Do you "chew your cud" before you do something? Or do you do something first and then think about it?

When people say they "cannot stomach" something, then they really, really don't like it. When people say they can't stomach a person, then they don't like that person. Is there any kind of music or movie or sport that you can't stomach?

> ? **APPLY**
> Is there a saying in your language about eating? Do you think this saying is always right?

After You Read

Write T (True) or F (False).

1 _____ Animal waste is good for some things.

Video
2 _____ The chameleon only eats large animals.

3 _____ The Komodo dragon is bigger than the Gila monster.

4 _____ The cow digests its food very quickly.

Video
5 _____ All animals digest food in their stomachs.

6 _____ The proboscis monkey eats the same food the cow eats.

7 _____ The hummingbird and the chameleon have long tongues.

8 _____ The Komodo dragon is dangerous to people.

Video
9 _____ Snakes chew their food before they swallow it.

10 _____ Tiger scat can have little parts of animals in it.

Complete the Sentences

Complete the sentences with the correct words from the box.

chew	digest	energy	saliva	stomach	swallow	tongue

1 In the _____ , food changes into

_____ for the body.

2 Teeth _____ food.

3 The _____ moves food around in the mouth.

4 Bodies _____ food to get the energy they

need.

5 _____ in the mouth makes food wet so it is

easy to _____ .

Choose the Correct Animal!

Write the name of the animal in the correct space.

blue whale   chameleon   cow   hummingbird   koala

1 _____ dung is good for the soil.

2 The mouth of the _____ is called a beak.

3 The _____ has a tongue as long as its body.

4 The baby _____ eats the waste of its mother.

5 Fifty people can stand on the tongue of a

_____ .

? DISCUSS

Do you know anybody who uses waste to help grow plants? What kind of waste do they use? What kind of plants do they grow? Do they eat the food they grow?

Answer Key

Words to Know, page 4
1 c **2** a **3** d **4** b

Words to Know, page 5
1 swallow **2** tongue **3** digest **4** stomach **5** energy
6 waste **7** bite **8** chew **9** saliva

Analyze, page 7
Possible answer: Birds fly a lot, so they need a lot of food.

Evaluate, page 9   *Answers will vary.*

Video Quest, page 11
The Komodo dragon is much bigger than the Gila monster.

Video Quest, page 13
It has a stomach with many small parts.

Analyze, page 17
All are good for the soil.

Video Quest, page 19
The tiger had not digested all of the samber deer.

Apply, page 21   *Answers will vary.*

True or False?, page 22
1 T **2** F **3** T **4** F **5** F **6** F **7** T **8** T **9** F **10** T

Complete the Sentences, page 22
1 stomach / energy **2** chew **3** tongue **4** digest
5 Saliva / swallow

Choose the Correct Animal!, page 23
1 Cow **2** hummingbird **3** chameleon **4** koala
5 blue whale